Grizzly

REFLECTIONS

REFLECTIONS *of the* WILDERNESS SERIES

by

KEN L. JENKINS

ICS BOOKS, INC.

Merrillville, Indiana

Dedication

I dedicate this book to the memory of Bob Smith. He realized a dream as he accompanied me into grizzly country for the last chapter of this book and the final adventure of his life. His constant encouragement and long-time friendship will never be forgotten.

Grizzly Reflections

Copyright © 1995 by Ken L. Jenkins

10 9 8 7 6 5 4 3 2 1

Printed in Singapore

Published by:
ICS Books, Inc.
1370 E. 86th Place
Merrillville, IN 46410
800-541-7323

Library of Congress Cataloging-in-Publication Data

Jenkins, Ken L.
    Grizzly reflections / Ken L. Jenkins.
       p. cm. — (Reflections of the wilderness series)
    ISBN 1-57034-012-9
      1. Grizzly bear. 2. Grizzly bear—pictorial works. I. Title. II. Series.
QL737.C27J45 1995
599.74'446—dc20   95-2553
                                            CIP

Table of Contents

Acknowledgments

Many thanks to those who live in grizzly country and share so much with so many. A special thanks to Mike and Robin Munsey for many miles of great adventure out of their lodge on Kodiak. A sincere thank-you to Wally and Jerine Cole, who have become like family as they share the very best of Denali National Park.

Preface

I n the hearts of those who truly love to disappear into wild places, nothing generates a more unique response than spotting the imprint of a bear paw in the trail. The anticipation of what might be found ahead adds a flavor of suspense unmatched by other experiences.

There is no conditioning for staying calm when confronted by this natural occurrence. Those who walk with bears often accept this sighting as a confirmation of the quality of the area in which they travel. The caution that should be observed when traveling in grizzly country is not to be taken lightly, though common sense and knowledge lead to safety. For most of my life I have chosen to travel in bear country for the reason that grizzlies exist in some of the most isolated and untouched wilderness areas in North America. My second reason, which quickly became my first, is that I marvel at the strength and intelligence of these mighty mammals and I love to observe them respectfully anytime I can. My many years of watching and photographing grizzlies have given me an appreciation for the tolerance that they show toward humans and I have developed a deep concern for the future of this wonderful creature. From Muir to Murie, the great naturalists of the past have been deeply impressed with the behavior of the grizzly. In my years of encountering grizzlies, many experiences stand above the rest. Each bear is a milestone in my love for nature and an education in appreciating wild places.

*I*f man is to coexist in harmony with nature, he must accept the responsibility of providing sanctuary for all that wilderness requires. In the truest heartland of wilderness stands the noble and magnificent grizzly. His only desire is to roam free and to occupy that vital role in the web of life for which he was created. Would this be too much to ask from the very symbol of healthy wildlands?

—Ken Jenkins, written after fifteen years of observing the grizzly
in the most remote corners of North America

Introduction

The silhouettes of giant evergreens protrude above the heavy morning fog. We have powered our boat twenty miles down this deep protected bay and now the silence is only broken by the wail of the dipping kittiwakes and arctic terns. Transferring into the whaler we motor to shallow water, cutting the engine and allowing the tide to carry us a few feet at a time. Within a hundred yards of shore we step out into the emerald waters and sink into the soft clam beds surrounded by waving grasses. In places our hip waders are tested as we pull the boat behind us in an attempt to be silent. The light is breaking through the mist when the first forms appear along the tidal flats. The sow and cubs have wandered far from shore searching for coho salmon coming into the mouth of the stream. Minute by minute the water deepens and the cubs begin to whine as they swim behind their wading mother. Our crew has moved into the shadow of the tree line as we spot more bears fishing the approaching waters. A crash in the dense brush behind us is a reminder that other bears have fed and are bedding down very near to our position. Walking on larger flattened rocks we move down the shore to gain access to the point where we can watch oncoming bear traffic. A step forward prompts an explosion of movement from the grassy bluff to our left. We freeze in our tracks as a mature bald eagle whooshes just over our heads. This will happen repeatedly on the walk to the point. There are many isolated spots on earth where only bears and eagles guard the beaches. In these rugged and remote regions the circle is yet unbroken. Everything is interdependent. The finest of each species seems to be represented here, whether it be the cross fox that searches for spawned-out salmon or the comical sea otter that patrols offshore. To be a part of such balance is a humbling experience and no matter how often I spend time in grizzly country, I take nothing for granted. The bear on the cover of this book reflected in the tidal pool as I watched from twenty yards away. Throughout the following pages are bears in their natural habitat. Each bear was aware of my presence, though never displayed aggression. Reflecting on those moments is among the great highlights of my life.

CHAPTER ONE

Bear Facts

The grizzly often traverses open, brush-covered terrain. In an attempt to reach the top of this slope in northern Montana, I gained greater respect for the strength and endurance of these bears. What appeared "open" became impassable tangles of undergrowth. A bear could conceivably travel through and feed along this slope in complete camouflage. There were the obvious signs that grizzlies were using the area regularly. Digging, tracks, droppings, and daybeds marked the home range of the bears. Though a grizzly may travel twenty to thirty miles in his search for food, many ideal home ranges contain foods that are sufficiently dispersed to allow the grizzly to remain year-round in a smaller area. It was clear that in this early autumn season, this slope belonged to the grizzly.

Depending on sex and maturity, a grizzly can weigh from 325 to 850 pounds yet remain completely hidden as he moves through willows and brush. Morning light had just warmed the ridge as this large male appeared seemingly out of nowhere. Grizzlies are known for minding their own business while being keenly aware of their territory. Intruders are seldom tolerated and reactions vary. This fellow sniffed the air, pinpointed my location, and continued to browse on soapberries, eventually disappearing into the thick vegetation.

A female grizzly always knows the location of her cub but the reverse is not always true. This young cub anxiously looked into the forest in an attempt to keep his mother's scent fresh. The sow had stopped by the shore of the river as if to tell the cub to stay in that spot. Cubs find many ways to pass the time and in the case of this bear, a fish bone kept his attention until the female bear came back to retrieve her offspring. The situation called for quiet observation on my part so as not to disturb the cub and bring the mother charging back to the scene to investigate.

In July this sow had two very healthy "cubs of the year." Possibly this was her first litter and she had not learned to be attentive. The salmon choked the river and several bears were tolerating each other due to the abundant food source. The second cub was dark brown and blended well into the shoreline. As the sow waded into the river to fish, the cubs stayed in shallow water. The darker cub followed the sow down the river but much too close to a large male bear. In one swift move the male grabbed the cub in his mouth and threw him near the shore. The drama ended at the edge of the woods with the sow roaring and the blond cub whining at her side. Losing a cub was a very hard lesson for this sow and when I returned to the river in early September, she kept the blond cub constantly in her shadow. The laws of nature are not based on what I feel is fair but on what it takes to survive. The sow will be careful with her cubs in coming years and perhaps the surviving cub that witnessed this event will be much more alert and cautious. The result will be, I'm sure, a stronger instinct to survive, and thus a more stable grizzly population in the vicinity of this river.

The grizzly is a carnivore and it seems appropriate to think of this animal as one in constant stalk of prey. In truth, he cannot capture enough food to sustain himself and must turn to vegetation for a more dependable diet. In this view across Moose Creek drainage in Denali, Alaska, bears can be spotted on a regular basis. In June, the tender grasses provide the nourishment necessary to maintain their bulk and satisfy their hunger. In addition to the tremendous amount of plants they take, we have often observed the bears gorging themselves on the carrion of winter-killed caribou or chasing the emerging arctic ground squirrels.

CHAPTER TWO

River of Bears

As I sat on the porch of my cabin I could see six to eight bears at any given time as they fished the Brooks River in Katmai, Alaska. A bluff in front of me blocked my view of the marshes fifty yards out. The sloshing of water and brushing of willows let me know that a bear was coming back from the river and very near to my position. Before I could raise up from my chair, the bulk of a large grizzly filled the ridge only thirty feet away. My only recourse at this point was to watch and wait so as not to alarm the bear. He stared at me for a few seconds then sat down and began to pull up large clumps of grass. He fed for nearly an hour while giving me occasional glances to verify my lack of movement. When another bear treaded through the marsh farther out, the scent prompted my visitor to move along quickly. The experience had been rewarding and exciting.

Katmai National Park in southwestern Alaska is perhaps the best place in the world to safely observe grizzlies as they fish for salmon along the mile-and-a-half stretch of the Brooks River. It will be interesting to see what the future holds for this small segment of a seventeen-hundred-square-mile park. When I first arrived in 1979, there was a sleepy little camp where mostly fishermen came to fish for salmon and other native fish species. A handful of bear watchers gathered throughout the day at the waterfall to share a bench and to watch the fishing tactics of the bears. Today several hundred people visit the Brooks River section of the park each year with the intention of watching bears. There are days when thirty to forty bears are present on the river. Two platforms allow observers to view key bear-fishing areas without blocking the paths of the animals. So far the intelligent grizzly has tolerated this sit-uation in a remarkable way and without incident or injury. Hopefully those with great foresight will further preserve this sanctuary in the best interest of the bears.

In grizzly country the path of least resistance is usually a bear trail. Bears have used the same trails through the forest for hundreds of years. On this bear trail and many similar ones, I have recorded evidence of bear behavior such as rubbing trees, making "belly" holes, and digging. In addition to these observations, I have met several bears along the trail and others bedded along the path.

Sockeye salmon fill the streams of Alaska from July into August. The bears depend on this feast to provide the bulk that carries them through the long winters. A bear can put on up to three hundred pounds in the course of the summer. Large bears weigh over a thousand pounds and can stand up to nine feet tall.

Like any good fisherman, this bear stood at the mouth to assess the number of fish moving into the river. The coastal grizzlies have learned to tolerate each other well in order to participate in the annual feasts. If he thinks fishing is better from the other side of the river, the bear will ponder the situation as he moves up along the fast-moving stream. When he does enter the water, he may float the stream with only his nose and eyes below the surface. Fishing tactics vary from bear to bear and success is limited to the persistent. From the observer's point of view, a bear fishing can be quite comical but his efforts are very serious.

Having observed numerous bears on many rivers, it is obvious to me that bears hate to get water in their ears. I have seen only a couple of bears on Brooks River who have adopted a style of fishing that sends them diving for their meal. Others search the pools and shallows in addition to floating the stream. The tactic is always to swim with nose and eyes just beneath the surface. When water accidentally seeps into the ears, the bear will shake his head aggressively to expel the unwelcome water.

A prime fishing spot above the falls is staked out at early light. Throughout the morning the spot is challenged, causing growls and roars that can be heard above the crashing of the waterfall. Bears use lots of body language when they interact in close quarters.

When several fish begin to jump the falls, one to five bears line up to try and snag their prey from midair. This young bear waited patiently for a fish to jump in his direction. Fish biologists say that it takes an average of five jumps for a salmon to cross a substantial waterfall. Often the bear gazed in the direction of the last fish that jumped while a second fish jumped just beside him. After much waiting and several close calls, a fish leaped high and just across the jaws of the waiting bear. In a lightning-fast movement he snatched the fish in his teeth and waded to a favorite rock to enjoy his catch.

CHAPTER THREE

Inland Habitat

These two siblings were content to spend a third year together. Probably weaned in early summer, they hunted and played together constantly. With a very short autumn and with winter coming on rapidly, the two will most likely den together as well. Just after this observation on a blueberry-covered slope, the bears located a small beaver pond and began to chase and dunk one another.

A food cache on the tundra is somewhat of a necessity for those who live in grizzly country. The legs are often wrapped in tin to prevent bears from climbing and ladders are removed after the cache is used. By storing food and items that would attract the bears, temptations are removed and bears move on to their natural diet. Often when a bear finds food in a dwelling used by humans, he will remain in that area and revisit that site often.

Bears love blueberries! As I "graze" along the slopes of the great North, it is an autumn delight to feast on the sweet berries. In many places the fruit is ground cover and seldom have I returned from bear watching that my knees were not dotted with purple. The bears are quite interesting in their berry picking. Rather than strip large branches of berries, they carefully pluck their prize a few berries at a time. Grizzlies begin to feed on blueberries before they ripen and as early as mid-July. However, in a great crop year, the bears completely depart from feeding on grasses by late August.

As far as the eye can see is true wilderness and prime bear country. After fifteen years of visiting Denali National Park in the heart of Alaska, I am convinced of the valuable sanctuary this park provides for grizzlies. The great naturalist Adolph Murie studied the grizzly in what was then Mount McKinley National Park for twenty-five summers. His conclusions were summarized in the following statement made in 1970: "Much of the mystique surrounding grizzlies may never be dispelled, and perhaps this is good, as long as we maintain a reverence for the continued existence of bears and preserve areas such as McKinley National Park in such a way that they may continue to live without harassment by man."

CHAPTER FOUR

Ideal Habitat

Afognak Wilderness is a vast, rugged region off the northeast coast of Kodiak Island in Alaska. Only a handful of people have chosen to live in this beautiful but untamed area. Travel on Afognak is best accomplished by taking a boat to a desirable entry point and following a river in at low tide. The underbrush is thick and in many places impassable, but the rewards for all efforts are unequalled. This too is prime bear country as I was soon to find out.

Roy Randall owns Afognak Wilderness Lodge and is truly a backcountry guide. He has carved his home out of the existing forest and has adapted to the land in a way that becomes obvious the minute you reach his dock. In addition to being self-sufficient, Roy knows wildlife and how they think. I came to his lodge to find an example of pure wilderness and I was not disappointed. It was mid-September and hints of cooler weather had begun to blow across the gulf. Only two fishermen shared the camp with me so plans were flexible each day.

There was a day when we motored around the huge island to a secluded inlet and climbed through the dense forest where a small inflatable boat had been

cached on a lakeshore. The motor went out in the middle of the lake and in the midst of a blowing storm. As we bobbed along the waves with engine parts on the vinyl floor of the Zodiac, I scanned the shore for bears. Most of the air had leaked out of the boat as we made the opposite shoreline. The path by the river was a bear trail and remains of freshly caught salmon littered the path. The river banks were rugged and steep. Making our way around a bend in the stream I saw wilderness paradise before me. The river broke over moss-covered boulders. The froth of the cascade formed the surface of a whirlpool below. Shadows of silver salmon moved near the fern-rich shoreline. The view upstream was a tunnel of the richest plant life. Trees had fallen across the water in many places and each was draped with the same golden mosses that coated most every branch in the forest. As I knelt on the bear trail to absorb all this beauty, I noticed the large tracks beside me. I had arrived here alone as Roy stayed back to repair our raft. This overwhelming experience affected all my senses. The earthen smells were heavy from the decaying matter of the forest that gave life to hundreds of other plants. The cool mist was a perfect complement to such a tranquil scene and the only sounds were singing birds and muffled rumblings of water.

The following day on Afognak, I was dropped off with my gear at the mouth of another river a few miles from camp. The day was spent along the river and on connecting streams and small lakes. In the evening I started my trek back to shore for a pickup.

Eagles commonly screamed from the treetops as I passed below. Every movement beside me caught my eye. The tide had caused the river to rise and my entry path was now covered. I moved further into the forest while following the river. Through the brush I spotted a young bear fishing but moving away from me. A second bear searched the rising tide for incoming salmon. The breeze was in my face and I moved along quietly before the second bear caught wind of me. If you have ever had that feeling of someone or, in this case, something watching you, then you can directly relate to the feeling that I was having as I moved downstream. I practiced the use of peripheral vision as I spread my line of sight across the dense

forest and even to the opposite bank
of the river. I thought of how fortu-
nate I was to be alone in such an
unspoiled place and of all that I
wanted to record in my journal that
night. Still I searched for the one that
eluded me but was surely out there
watching. The day was almost gone
and I was less than a half mile from
the mouth of the river. The sun had
turned the water golden on the surface and I stopped to record this liquid beauty.
As I focused on the river's surface, a small head appeared and immediately disap-
peared. Had this been my company as I hiked along the river? The head reappeared
and remained just six feet away. A harbor seal had come in from the bay to fish and
for some reason found my presence quite unusual. He had followed me for some

time just offshore, disappearing at my slightest glance. I found comfort in his company and he stayed until dark, when I heard the distant motor of my return boat ride to camp. The bears broke branches as they moved through the woods behind me and on to the river to fish. It was a confirmation of the many wonderful days spent in grizzly country. There is always more to see and experience in bear country because bears truly do live in the richest habitats in North America.

When the last light of evening reflects off the water, the bears often walk the shoreline. Whether heading back to a favorite bedding spot or investigating the fishing, the silhouette of a bear along the river is the perfect way to end the day.

In the northern sections of our continent, grizzlies live and interact with the caribou. In the scene of tundra above, the gray segment represents a gravel bar, which is a thoroughfare for all wildlife, including the grizzly. A caribou can outrun a bear in this area but may be overtaken in dense willows and alder. This autumn perspective reveals ideal habitat for the grizzly. He feeds on the blueberries here and beds down in the heavy brush. The caribou feeds on the mosses on these ridges and beds on open slopes.

CHAPTER FIVE

Walking in Bear Country

Hiking in bear country can be the greatest joy of an outdoor lover's career as long as one practices common sense and obeys the regulations set up for backcountry use. Bears are not lurking behind every bush waiting for an unsuspecting hiker. Given the chance, any wild bear will flee from sight when he realizes that you are in the area.

There are exceptions to this rule, which I have experienced, but they are unusual situations. Knowing what to do in bear country is a prerequisite for going there.

30

Early one July morning I broke camp and headed through the woods alone. I was on my first solo trip through several of Alaska's national parks and forests. (Backpacking or dayhiking alone in grizzly country is not recommended.) About three miles from camp I began to smell a strong odor and a couple of times I had heard branches cracking some distance away. In another eight miles I noticed a large bare patch to the left of the trail and about a hundred yards away. I waded through the low vegetation and was amazed to find an area that appeared to have been excavated by heavy equipment. About the same time I noticed the jawbone of a moose along with other fragments of the kill. I assumed that more than one bear had fought for the kill resulting in downed trees and turned-under ground. Everything I knew about grizzly bears burying their kill then came to mind and I suspected that the bear responsible might be very near. As I moved away, I heard crashing brush and popping jaws. A medium-sized bear stood up by a tree and smacked the tree a couple of times and again popped his jaws. I moved away slowly and looked back constantly until I saw the bear turn and crash through the woods in the opposite direction.

KATMAI NATIONAL PARK, ALASKA

The moose is a valuable part of any ecosystem. In areas where moose and grizzlies share the same habitat, moose lose a high percentage of their calves. Predation is due in part to the ability of a bear, or a wolf pack in many cases, to separate the cow moose from one of her calves. One-on-one the cow can defend herself against the grizzly. With one calf she can usually head off the attacks of the bear or wolf. If one of the calves panics, however, she cannot concentrate her efforts in two directions and often the calf is lost. My experience has taught me to have great respect for the cow moose and to give her a wide berth. One evening we witnessed a cow being charged by a grizzly in Denali National Park. The cow partially stood on her hind legs and kicked the bear swiftly in the front quarters. The bear rolled several yards and did not repeat the charge.

One afternoon as I returned to Brooks River in Alaska, I decided to walk along the river where the bears were fishing rather than take the forest trail that led to the waterfall. (There is safety in numbers and it is wise to travel in bear country in parties of two or three.) As I walked through tall grasses, I noticed very fresh fish in the path and seeping bear tracks. I was relieved to reach an opening just before the falls, though my intention was to pass by the falls and to the mouth of the river. There were no bears beneath the falls so I proceeded along the path upstream. The wind was blowing slightly as I topped the falls. (Hiking in windy conditions in known bear country makes it difficult for bears to locate your scent and increases the possibility of a surprise.) Out of the tall grass a sow stood and stared without a growl or pop of jaw. Fortunately her cub was behind her and began to whine and scamper up the river. The sow dropped to the ground and moved slowly toward the cub. Three conditions had made this a very dangerous situation. The bear was a female with a cub, the wind had carried away my scent, and the falls had drowned out my approaching footsteps. It was a lesson learned and a mistake that will not be repeated.

A bear walking directly toward you does not qualify as aggressive behavior. This healthy specimen met me on the trail and yet continued in my direction. Bear experts recommend raising one's hands and calmly speaking to allow the bear to know what you are. Slowly and steadily back away from the bear. If the bear continues down the trail, he is very likely looking for a place to exit or this is perhaps his path. In this case look for a place to step away from the trail and let the bear know exactly where you are. (Never run, speak loudly, or do anything to excite the bear.)

CHAPTER SIX

Island Paradise

Bears are opportunists and in places like Kodiak there is a literal feast available each time the tide comes and goes. Above, several bears tolerate each other on the tidal flats as incoming waters from Larsen Bay bring salmon to the mouths of freshwater streams. The water will eventually push the bears to shore, where berries and grasses will supplement their diet. Some of the largest grizzlies in the world live on Kodiak Island.

There are several places on earth that seem so pristine, so perfectly landscaped by the forces of nature, that one immediately feels drawn into the heart of all that this area has to offer. Kodiak Island in south central Alaska is that place to me. I have witnessed no other landscape so lush yet so rugged. It is the emerald island with vertical slopes of deepest green, snowcapped highlands dotted with crystal-clear lakes, and hundreds of miles of coastline dissected by a multitude of rivers and streams. This land is so remote that a floatplane is the only practical approach to most areas.

A few years ago I heard about Mike and Robin Munsey, who operate a small bear camp an hour's flight from the town of Kodiak. When I flew out to Munsey's Bear Camp, I saw the most beautiful country I had ever witnessed. Our small float-plane flew low across the passes where we spotted mountain goats and bear. As we banked for our landing, eagles circled the camp and kittiwakes exploded into the air from nearby rookeries. The Munseys were waiting for us at the dock.

37

Park Munsey, Mike's father, was a master bear-guide known throughout the world. Mike and Robin are specialists in bears as well as in the flora and fauna of the area. Growing up on this island of bears in this very remote location has given Mike a unique ability to understand the mighty Kodiak bear. Each morning we take his steel-hulled trawler down the bay to begin another bear adventure. As we transfer to a smaller boat, we begin to see bears moving in the distance in the low light. The walk in to shore must be a quiet approach and with luck the wind will blow in our direction so the bears remain on the flats. Today we have four people with every intention of remaining silent. We choose our steps carefully until we reach an ideal viewing point. Dozens of eagles have flown out over our heads, and an awakened bear crashed into the alders just beyond us. A cross fox strolled right up to us and another fox waded well out onto the flats to retrieve an abandoned fish head. We watched for hours as bears walked very close to us and then into the rising tide. As the deep green water rose, the bears and even the fox reflected a mirror image as they fished in front of us.

Above, a sow and her two spring cubs approach the tidal flats to fish. The mother bear will eventually share her catch with her begging cubs but every moment is a lesson in life for the young bears. The tide comes in quickly and the cubs protest loudly as they are forced to swim behind their mom. She will bring them in only when she senses that the fishing is no longer productive.

One of the miracles of nature is surely the story of the salmon. Born in shallow depressions in wilderness rivers and lakes, these young fish swim downstream and out to sea in huge schools. According to the species, in three to seven years they instinctively seek the freshwater rivers that they were born in. As they enter these waters the cycle becomes complete. They lay eggs and fertilize them and die. Nothing is wasted in nature and that truth is evident when thousands of salmon complete their life's work. The bears are obsessed with gorging on this rich source of protein. Eagles swoop down from overhanging branches to take their share while foxes, wolves, mink, and otter share in the feast. These sockeye salmon have turned scarlet red on reaching fresh water.

Many times the only way to walk upstream is to get in the water. With hip waders I had made my way a couple of miles up a fast-moving stream choked with salmon. In places if I had had something to grip, I could have walked on top of the salmon, they were so thick. In the distance I could hear gulls crying and several flew up just above the tall grasses in the bend ahead. This is almost always a sign that a bear is fishing. I moved out of the river into the grasses and onto a small cut bank. The bear was on the opposite side of the stream with his head and nose beneath the surface. Several times he rose out of the water looking directly upstream as the water poured from his mouth like a browsing moose. He must have smelled another bear farther upstream because he continued intently to stare upstream immediately after rising out of the water. I positioned my gear to record the moment. As I looked through the viewfinder I found the bear was staring directly at *me*. I picked up my gear and quietly left the area. (Never look directly at a grizzly. In bear language this could mean a threat and could provoke the bear to anger.)

41

In coastal regions, the mouth of a river can be disguised in tall grasses. This cover provides comfortable passage for the bears and a place to bed down after feeding. Often when the bears are feeding, the eagles light on nearby driftwood, hoping to snag a fish in the shallows. Walking through these grasses keeps one's adrenaline pumping as each step can flush a group of gulls, a bald eagle—or a sleeping bear.

The tolerance that bears have for each other while the fish are running is quite amazing. This acceptance only goes so far, however, and when that invisible circle is invaded the intruder is quickly dispelled. This young bear moved much too close to a sow with her young. When she lashed out at him, he did not stop running until he reached the shore.

CHAPTER SEVEN

Gaining Perspective

It is easy to lose perspective in a popular bear-viewing area like Katmai National Park. This park on the Alaska Peninsula occupies 4.1 million acres yet 90 percent of the activity is concentrated along a mile-and-a-half stretch of river.

Early one morning I walked out of camp through the alders into the poplar and birch stands and several miles onto a ridge overlooking the spruce forest. It was from this vantage point that this extremely rich area came into focus for me. The sound of the river was so muffled that it took a back seat to the cool breeze blowing lightly through the spruce boughs. Quickly you realize that all of this area is bear country as well as wolf country, wolverine country, and rich habitat for dozens of other mammals that occupy wilderness in its finest form. For a period of time there are no floatplanes buzzing overhead, no hikers screaming, "Hey bear!" and no rangers pleading with fishermen and photographers to keep their distance from the bears. It is peaceful here just the way the wilderness should be. The bears have passed this way recently, as evidenced by their digging and droppings. A spruce grouse was quietly foraging along the bearberry-covered slope in front of me. A red squirrel sounded in the spruce above me. In the distance the waters of Naknek Lake were calm and the length of the turquoise arm separated the forest from the rugged mountains beyond. I knew that as far as I could see the grizzly was master of his domain. As Murie had said, he owns no natural "over-lord." The bear has no enemy except man and is king of all animals over this 4-million-acre range. I had walked through the Valley of Ten Thousand Smokes and followed the tracks of the bear. I had flown over the glaciers and seen the bears digging at their base. There was no part of the forest nor was there a river or lake that the bear did not know and move through. The picture was much clearer as I walked back to camp. The abundance of food creates an opportunity to view the bears, but it is the grizzly that extends the compliment to man in allowing him to observe and coexist during the days of plenty. It is a mutual respect that I hope continues, because if man betrays the trust the bear will unfortunately lose.

KATMAI NATIONAL PARK, ALASKA

This is one of several cabins in Brooks Camp facing the river. The cabins are comfortable, though bears regularly frequent the entire camp area.

The wolf is a major part of the Katmai ecosystem. On three occasions as I sat on the banks of the river waiting for the bears to return to a favored fishing hole, a wolf came to the river to drink and to survey the area. He always and immediately sensed my presence and departed. There is photographic evidence of wolves standing atop the same falls that the bears use. Their intentions are the same—to take advantage of this rich food source.

There are intervals of heavy salmon-running in the rivers and bears adapt to this in various ways. Many search for a time and return to daybeds if the fish are not abundant. The smaller bears tend to move into the rivers when fewer bears are present. On occasion, a very large bear efficient at catching fish will find an island or boulder near the best fishing spots and rest until activity resumes. This large bear had been king of the river in years past. Fifteen years ago I came to know him as Diver. The bear biologist named him for his unusual manner of obtaining fish in that he totally submerges for extended periods of time and frequently surfaces with a fish. I must admit becoming very fond of this bear over my many visits through the years. His tolerance toward humans is unequalled and his temperament toward other, younger bears is mild in comparison to that of his larger peers.

The salmon that spawn and die along the rivers are often in a state of decay. Some bears are quite content to feast on the very dead fish as seen above. Bear biologists believe that the tapeworms developed in the bear are eliminated by the bears' feeding on the blue mud from the river bottom. The bear below inspects a clump of this mud as if to choose just the right bite.

Each summer as I return to the salmon streams, I search for bears that I have observed in the past. As the summer ends I pay special attention to the aging bears, always wondering if they will make it through the winter. This old fellow had a broken foot and several deep battle wounds.

To remain a dominant bear requires constant exertion of power and the appearance of a strong and capable ruler. In general, bears are solitary creatures and attempts by other bears to invade their space are met with fierce growls and possible attacks. Injuries that occur can be long lasting or fatal, though the grizzly is quite resilient. In many of my observations, a bear has come away limping from a fight and may disappear from the presence of other bears for a period of time, then return when he knows he can handle the obvious challenges of competing for food and territory.

Often this bear would sit and watch the ground squirrels scamper near his den. After a while he began to graze on nearby grasses, moving closer to the small mammals with each bite. In an explosion of speed he chased them under a large boulder that he easily rolled away to give him access to one of his favorite foods.

CHAPTER EIGHT

Remaining Wild

Our parklands in North America provide the last stronghold for the noble grizzly. If we regard our parks as systems of interrelated animals, plants, and habitats, we will put an emphasis on naturalness with a minimum of human interference. If this happens, the grizzly will continue to rule his domain. It was stated over forty years ago: "Let us be guardians rather than gardeners."

May the track of the grizzly always be evident in wild places and may the path of man always yield the right of way to him.